LEFT AT THE POST

To whom it may concern

LEFT AT THE POST

Evan Jones

University of Queensland Press

First published 1984 by University of Queensland Press
P.O. Box 42, St Lucia, Queensland, Australia

Typeset by University of Queensland Press
Printed in Australia by The Dominion Press–Hedges and Bell, Melbourne

Distributed in U.K., Europe, the Middle East, Africa, and the
Caribbean by Prentice Hall International, International Book
Distributors Ltd, 66 Wood Lane End, Hemel Hempstead, Herts.,
England

Distributed in the U.S.A. and Canada by Technical Impex
Corporation, 5 South Union Street, Lawrence, Mass. 01843 U.S.A.

Published with the assistance of the Literature Board of the Australia Council

Cataloguing in Publication Data

National Library of Australia

Jones, Evan, 1931–
   Left at the post.

   ISBN 0 7022 1717 4.
   ISBN 0 7022 1718 2 (pbk.).

   I. Title.

A821'.3

Library of Congress

Jones, Evan, 1931–
   Left at the post.

   I. Title.
PR9619.3.J686L4   1984   821   83-23262
ISBN 0-7022-1717-4
ISBN 0-7022-1718-2 (pbk.)

Acknowledgments

Most of these poems have appeared severally in *Quadrant*, *Helix*, the *Age*, the *Sydney Morning Herald*, *Westerly*, the *Canberra Times*, *Australian Poets Catalogue*, the *Victorian Law Institute Journal*, the *Times Literary Supplement*, *Scripsi*, the *Bulletin*, the *Poetry Book Society's Christmas Supplement*, 1980, and *Poems in Honour of James McAuley*.

Contents

Nursery Rhyme

for Peter Steele

When they first jauntily agreed
the bells, the vows, the rice, whatever
to marry, make themselves one indeed
witty, touching, deft and clever
did the stars shiver, did the earth bleed?

One two three their children were born
bells, holy water, precious gifts
clever, stubborn and all alone
handsome their habits, handsome their shifts
and the wide, wide world was green.

She wandered that way, he went this
tickets for all the fairgrounds cheap
looking for whatever was.
and all the springs were bitter and deep
Their children learnt that life is loss.

Go to sleep, my pretty one, sleep:
nothing that is is just as it was:
nothing will keep, nothing will keep:
cross your true heart and weep for its loss.

A Letter from the House-Mouse to the Beavers

For Bruce and Brenda

What, after all, would you imagine that I'd
    be doing, the music on,
the dishes still to be washed, the bills unpaid,
    my books at home, the children
elsewhere, elsewhere, reviews still to be written?
    Grief's is a little atlas,
its countries coloured the light brown that declares
    deserted wastes, its covers
limp and dejected: mostly they stay closed now,
    though every now and then
a remembered detail draws me sharply back
    to study those odd, sad, bleached
configurations: crosses and place-names offer
    clues to forgotten campaigns,
triumphs and celebrations and lost cultures —
    How exquisite the work was
on that brooch, that sword, that buckler . . . with a sigh
    I close the book again, turn
to dish-washing, reading, cooking, reviewing,
    the trade of opinion and
indeed information — what, in short, for me
    makes some show of capable life.

Your picture-calendar for this year of grace,
    nineteen seventy-six,
displays nude women in frolic, unlikely
    conjunctions and risible
shifts in the dance: I see them hung up in shops.
    For me, this year has begun
as one where my dreams are lost upon waking;
    lost upon waking, too,
fear, anxiety — either I simply sail
    into dead calm, or if
tradewinds are blowing become the sentient
    student of dreams, old dreams,
conjectures, appraisals, rehearsals, reports.
    No-one of course can expect
to know everything, but some ones here and there
    have stabbed at it better than
I sometimes used to imagine managing —
    what lonely egocentrics
they must have been, alas! But now around me
    Bach weaves again that shining
web of perfect order which I can neither
    comprehend nor disbelieve.
My God! there I am at it again. It's time
    to go to bed and to dream
whatever I won't remember tomorrow,
when one bill after another becomes due.

Drinking with Friends

for Brian Buckley

We used to sit up until three or four
drinking whatever there was: the decor
was characteristically indiscriminate,
the company, those curious and articulate
about politics, art, psychology. It seemed
to me I stammered, others talked: I'm damned
if I can remember getting much of a hearing.
My friends remember me as domineering.

   Sing hey, sing hey for those yesterdays,
   the brilliant chat and its wanton ways,
   lost, of course, in a golden haze.
   It's nice to talk with old friends.

Commonly it's more comfortable now
with O.K. wines and breezier talk: somehow
things have increased and declined. But when the chatter
turns as it still will do to what things matter,
my helpless lack of dicta earns reproof:
haughty I'm thought, unamenable, aloof.
The only thing one never can imagine
is how one looks to others, with or without wine.

   Sing ho, sing ho for the silences:
   not one of us is as glib as he was
   before the whiff of defeat gave him pause.
   It's nice to talk with old friends.

A Birthday Poem

The only one with anything like
your mother's unsettling green eyes,
how long I have learned to love you, Rachel.

Everything's hard to make much sense of,
but if I were to give
any advice to a child of mine,
I'd say this much about staying alive:

lie low while you can, but if
you simply have to stand up
keep clear of the edge, or at the worst
be sure you have measured the drop —

and that's of course supposing
a high unbroken ground
with room to move and air so clear
you can see for years around.

Not everywhere is like that: you'll find
valleys cut like a scar
where the woods are thick, the water dead
and it's hard to know where you are:

this is the scary country
where bogles might be hiding —
move carefully, trust to your luck, but watch
anything smiling, scowling, gliding

or crumpling: they're all to hungry,
likely to gobble you up in a flash . . .
But even murk-wood is prettier than
the cities and ports where men go smash.

There more than ever you have to beware
and learn to follow your nose,
especially if you drift too near
to the rowdy spots where the good gang goes:

that's where you watch out for the hoods and dips,
the people who live on their nerves,
the suckers and the parasites
who eat out on whatever life serves.

Look out for the swingers, high-flyers, cool cats,
and if you just have to prowl
stay close to the zoo where the real tigers are
and look and blink like an owl.

Souvenir

for Talis Polis

Her first gift to me, in the stout cardboard box
of a city jeweller. I remember the shock
of disappointment when I unwrapped the tissue:
the plainest glass ash-tray, however impeccably new.
Then I put it on the gleaming black table in the flat
where she was to join me. It was elegant, Swedish,
                    something to marvel at.

Taking it from the dish-rack eleven years later, I think
as so often before how sadly scoured and chinked
it is, looking, just as it did for that first moment,
like the cheapest ash-tray that would draw no comment
in any suburban hotel. I put it, though,
on the battered cedar table in the house that she left
                    years ago.

Folk Tale

for Bob Priestley

What could he do, the oldest son,
but work on, work on
as the second son waxed drunk and fat
and the third son ran of course
into success, and that was that.
Get up, get up, old horse.

What could happen to the second son
but booze on, booze on,
as the youngest son grew callous and smart,
while the oldest son of course
kept drudging on with a stubborn heart.
Get up, get up, old horse.

What could happen to the youngest son
but to be well looked upon,
while the second son was damned for his failings,
and the oldest son of course
ran slow and steady and close to the railings.
Get up, get up, old horse.

What could happen to the youngest son
but to have no-one to lean upon
when he started to feel old and cold
and the second son felt no remorse
while the oldest son sold what could be sold.
Get up, get up, old horse.

What could happen to the second son
when his last puncheon was gone
and the candles failed and he started to shake,
and the oldest son of course
came to scold and bury and take.
Get up, get up, old horse.

What could happen to the oldest one
with two daughters and a son
as his flesh shrank and the skin grew loose:
his kinder knew just how to behave —
they slipped their knot and left a noose.
Get into the grave, get into the grave.

Another Music

Through urban uproar, through the steep silence of
    a solitude far removed from you,
whoever, whatever, wherever you are,
    come rifts of remembered harmony,
or half-remembered, to my unmusical
    mind, imagining, memory, or
the simple ghost that hearkens to sheer order.

Un-notable, fragmentary, inaudible
    when listened for, unaccountable,
it leads me carrolling through the quagmire of
    rememberance and introspection and
washing the bloody dishes, mostly glasses,
    which lie about me like the bright shards
bower-birds gather for no better reason.

Not that I know so much about bower-birds:
    their dance is display, mine solitude;
theirs leads to regeneration, mine now treads
    a singular quickstep to its end,
though common enough, and interweaving with
    pirouettes projected by the past
into forever. Maybe we'll dance again.

Genre Painting

for Leigh Astbury

"You know", she seems sadly to be saying, "I never
mean what I say"; his head is bowed. They sit forever
in yellows deepening glumly through green to black
in front of a rain-swept window, her crimson frock
and the bowl of pink roses low in the right-hand corner,
subdued though they are, all that the gazer can garner
against the sheer gloom of a perfectly minor painting,
lachrymose, accomplished, faintly haunting.

It's an inconspicious thing. It never would
catch more than the eyes of those who in vacant mood
drift into this tiny alcove, subdued, almost as if
the bravura of great art enhancing life
had left them havocked, needing to contemplate
something much less demanding, something so far from great
as this poor dated essay in painterly skill
and story-telling. The story holds them still.

Cezanne, El Greco, Breughel are far away; the nervous hands
are not like Dürer's. Though every upward line in the picture ends
broken in darkness, her eyes, his high and unmarked brow
betray a kind of innocence — till now
nothing has made or marred them: nothing at all
prompts us to wonder or outrage. But walking away one small
question remains, as if forever and ever: what belief
led to just such a dull meticulous rendering of grief?

The Wizard to Dorothy

Emerald City, 1974

If you just *have* to kill me
please do it with a gun,
and make quite sure for Christ's sake
the job's not left half-done.

And then don't tell my children
how wicked you are, and sad,
or somewhere not too far away
I'll go stark raving mad.

Just treat them as your own kids —
a lick, a smack, a hint —
and let them wander through the dreams
that I thought fit to print.

The Cavalryman's Lament

for Joseph Johnson

The horses strain towards the winning post
while we sit eating buttered toast and egg.
The Tank Command surveys the permafrost.

We check our tickets, count what we have lost
and put our hopes upon the second leg:
the horses strain towards the winning post

and everything's all wrong, the favourite tossed
by an ill-favoured, unsupported nag.
The Tank Command surveys the permafrost

and finds that German Leopards can do most —
so much indeed that they're inclined to brag.
The horses strain towards the winning post,

last bets, late fancies, all go by at last
and gross banausic fellows crack the keg.
The Tank Command surveys the permafrost,

the nicer chaps drift off towards the coast
to stretch their pensions, tout, bet as they beg
on horses straining towards the winning post.
The Tank Command surveys the permafrost.

Startled Glimpses

for Peter Kortschak

i Lullaby

Babby your mummy is eating the moon,
babby O babby she can't keep it down.
Babby O babby go to sleep.

Babby the moon is eating your mum,
she looks so golden, babby, babby,

babby, babby,

your father is trying to swallow the sun
and the light is blood-red all over town:
it looks for Godsake just like dawn.

Babby O babby go to sleep.

ii The poets, bless them

Like looking for a needle in a haystack
the ceaseless search for herself: so I,
sitting at table, thought. All round, the talk
trickled like watered wine: the poets, bless them,
were, present as always, busily turning
the future into the past, the past into
the future, and so on. None of it will end
while you, dear reader, sit there bemused as I was.

iii **Wednesday's child** Mt Martha in November

Remembering loneliness, I remember
a vacant Sunday wandering round King's Cross —
hung-over, far from home —
the wife whom I loved and lost still in the future,
still in the future the distant daughters
I've not seen now for six days
nor shall see today nor tomorrow.

I should of course look forward to seeing them soon,
but lost in this springy maze
who on earth could muster
a fifty-mile far-away three-day gaze?

iv **The rough ride** For Frank Kellaway

"Stay with it, kid" was all he said —
so I hung on, half-dead.
That was an age ago, and yet
I'm still hanging on and I won't let
go till it stops, if I can help it.
I don't know any way to stop it.

v **Merlin's song**

No witch on her broomstick was more comely than
my lady on her bicycle,
no icicle

more unmelting than she.
I stand here rooted as a tree,
looking like a man.

vi Night walkers For D. E. Kennedy

We run, unlike the loud baboon,
between the marshes and the rocks
the gamut of abuse:
under the lucid lonely moon
as constant as the silly goose,
the sly monogamous fox.

vii After Adam Lindsay Gordon

Life feels mainly too like stone,
two things feel like froth:
kindness when one's all alone
and good luck to you both.

viii A good man lies where he falls

"Dote if you must on Richard the Lion-heart,
but Saladin would have cut him apart
before he could lift that great two-handed sword
— you will have to take my word"
said the middle-aged lonely man
staring into the dark,
wine lying beside him on the cane divan,
the pipe in his hand glowing dully, without spark.

ix Transcendental meditation

Look blankly at the map:
who takes his wisdom from
a country shaped like a trap?

x A dream of consolation For Dinny O'Hearn

Cheer up, it might never happen.
                    It would have happened anyway.
In twenty years, it will all seem the same.
Well, dear, you've lost the point, but not the game.
Well, that's his game: there are other games to play.

Sorry of course: what else is there to say?

xi Ars longa, vita brevis est?

Sometimes my life seems rather long,
my verses very short —
I hear the green world's swift laconic song:
O turn it up, old sport.

xii The hare and tortoise caper For Frank and Lorna Price

Some burn fast and some burn slow,
some fly high and some fly low:
whatever I've got, take what you need
and let me die at my own speed.

xiii A prayer for my mother's memory

Dear God, who else at last will understand
that that was always someone else, not me?
For ever and ever amen.

xiv Envoy

No-one left, thank God, to look
over my shoulder at my dreams.
Farewell.

xv Ah wilderness!

"Come on", said the middle-aged man, "I'm game:
I can do anything I ever could: there's nothing surer."
When it came to the point he was wrong: he could
                no longer put his name
to romantic slipshod bravura.

The One-eyed Giant

The one-eyed giant sat for years in his castle.
No-one could match him with weapons;
there was none who would choose to wrestle.

If he caused trouble to any-one
by eating too much mutton, that isn't recorded.
A bell rang when the meat was properly done,

the telly or the radio entertained him,
dish- and clothes-washers, vacuum cleaner
took care of him well, for which he blessed them.

He took pride in some things: he carved his meat
with a good Sabatier knife; if his clothes
were careless, he was careful about his feet —

no ostentation, certainly, but some
care for the sensitive sole, and flexibility.
Mainly, as a giant, he was very hum-drum.

No wonder then that Sir Cei and Sir Bedwyr,
out on one of their admirable murderous quests,
had little trouble in finding out from a neighbour

how to approach him: "we polish knives and boots."
He offers them dinner: they enter: in no time
they have his head off; then, while one loots,

the other plays and sings to his mandolin,
"It was all for the love of a lady."
God knows why the poor bastard let them in.

Poem just after midnight: summer: at home

for Leigh and Neta Astbury

For a moment, I heard the surge of waves
in the wind in the trees in my back-yard:
forty years collapsed for an instant.
Among my books and papers, secure
in a kind of reputation,
what takes my mind is wind, wind in the trees
and the vast rolling of water. When
my bones are washed quite white, who will
remember my patient efforts to mimic
in words the smaller rhythms
of private life with its rewards and frustrations?
Somebody might. It hardly seems to matter
as I listen again for the wind to toss the trees,
the whole stir of a world
moving away.

Bedtime Stories

for John Timlin

I

The children thank God are sleeping quietly
after a story from the Brothers Grimm.
The parents over wine, but with sobriety,
are talking about this. She says to him,

"Surely that irrational violence will
distort their lives, and the absurd
old superstitions slowly smother and kill
their growing sense of reality." In a word

the husband says "Yes." Neither would hit
anything larger, less noxious, than a fly.
They sit and sip and think of it a bit,
neither quite liking to ask the other why

they feed their children such pernicious stuff.
But Enid Blyton, or even Mary Grant Bruce?
Not culture at all. That isn't reason enough,
but even the gentlest people must make truce,

and so again, sober but slightly bemused,
they go to bed themselves, touch kindly, turn away
to several dreams, unhelpful and confused.
Tomorrow is going to be another day.

II

Vaguely besotted at last
by his three-decker novel,
sated also with port,
an ageing man slips to the level

where the book drops: light sleep:
no menacing whisper, no shout,
just something rather like life
flickering, fading out.

Shopping at Crittenden's

Each time I walked behind
a long-haired girl, delighted
by her swift shopping decisions.
Occasionally she'd turn
to talk about purchases, once
for a dinner we ate together.
Each time I bought a sausage
of preserved, compounded meat
for my large and lively neutered tabby.

I still live alone with the cat,
who still eats mainly the same
inexcusable mess, but bought now
elsewhere, and at rather less expense.

Instructions to a Servant

for Don Gunner

Since I'm retiring late again, dear Smith,
please try not to disturb me when you come.
The nest of papers and the books on myth

might best be left untouched. The bath shows scum:
the pantry needs more rat-bait: clear the sink:
there are some cob-webs in the living-room —

but otherwise, proceed just as you think.
After the dusting, washing-up and mopping
don't hesitate to give yourself a drink

if you can find one (I missed out on shopping).
That's almost all, but you might like to look
at some things in the garden before stopping:

there's a dark weed I rather think is hemlock
which chokes the parsley; and the pile of bones
in the far corner might with care and luck

submit to being cairned beneath the stones
from last year's digging. Little else to say.
I hope you and the world are well. Yours, Jones.

About the House

for my parents

I think perhaps it ought to be set up
when the children turn out after all
not to want it, as a sort of monument
like, say, Captain Cook's, Ann Hathaway's cottages.
Frankly, I still don't know where it will stop:
the garden is changing: I watch it. One wall
cries for a picture still beyond my discernment.
All that depends upon a sense of wages.

Looking around, I find I'm written clear
not only in what seems to me elegance —
almost everything now bears my taste's stamp —
but by a kind of meanness. No oak,
one piece of mahogany, one walnut, the rest cedar:
everything sound without extravagance.
Plainness is prevalent, though some kind of trump
is played with David Fitts' paintings and one rug

hung in a place of honour (neither silk nor antique).
Look here and you will find me. Of course
for most of my life I scorned things for themselves,
excepting always books, which I hoarded like a magpie:
but then at last I overwhelmingly took
to wanting my own place to be at peace,
at peace with my own. Empty cupboards, empty shelves
still mark the time when my wife bid it all goodbye,

taking the kids. How hollow it all seemed then!
But still there were things that needed changing,
nagging me just by being not yet accomplished.
I plugged away: it's at least a second home
to the kids now. To me again and again,
empty and all and needing re-arranging,
it seems in some ways all I ever wished,
the home I never had. My parents' home,

God bless them, was never a resting place,
never the centre of their attention: they
were busy fortune-building for their family. In
their seventies, they're home-bodies at last:
their house receives their grandchildren with grace,
they have a place for everything, a way
of taking their children and their children's children in
with cheer and comfort. On the other hand, alas,

the decor, the furniture, the furnishings, the fabric
of the house itself declare it all too roundly
no home to which I could ever retreat for more
than a brief visit: nervous, restless,
I want my own house with its dusky brick,
its shady disorderly garden: sadly,
I think that it and the children are what I have lived for,
all the rest epiphenomena, more or less.

Lullaby

Sleep, old thing: so far
as retrospection kens
nothing at all went wrong
since early morning when
everything went all right —
waking the kids and fussing,
getting them off to school:
soon it will happen again.

There, there's a certain grace:
turn over world, stars shift
while I hide my head in the pillow,
muttering soundlessly in a drift
a kind of litany to the great one:
let days so empty of face
come up as empty of nothing
that I can cope with; let

in the hypnagogic trance
some faces be recalled:
most of their eyes were blue:
some hazel, some brown
— but in the drift of words
they fade into abstraction, scold,
entreat, demur, or simply drown.
Only one name goes running on and on.

Sleep, old thing: how nice
not to have put up a black
all day: no insults, no secrets, no lies,
a bland unmemorable day,
its busyness smothering regret.
Dream what you like about your lady's eyes,
they'll be as clear as water,
                        as blue as your daughters'
when you wake up in paradise.

Out of Season

Tonight we do not play, messieurs,
mesdames, the time is out . . .
O all the music, all the games
and how we ran about
like cats and mice together!
  There is a shadow in the flames,
there is a colder weather,
all summer's fluent water cures,
the promenade, the slink, the flout,
touchings of one another

are gone with a roll of dice.

I.M. James McAuley

Jim, all your contradictions
are lucidly resolved now.
I write these words in homage
to the private man I loved.

A Commemoration of Professor Hope

Written for the opening of the A.D. Hope building
at the Australian National University, 7 July 1977.

Polyglot motley puzzle-minded man,
how the years yawn away! It scarcely seems
a wink since you woke from fantasy to fame,
and now your antic organdie of dreams
winces and settles to a classic. Can
this grand-stand witness that fleet gauzy game?

Scholar of monsters, sciences and magic,
lore of the folk and nit-wit nursery rhyme,
strait-faced you triumphed in the comi-tragic;
in your account of love and the erotic
the mandarin, the vulgar, the exotic
wedded mere bathos to the sheer sublime.

Cannon and chime salute the accessible.
Forgotten, far-off, and quite inaudible
the yearning ghost is on another way.
But no doubt there will be another message,
and those who celebrate these rites of passage
will gape tomorrow as they gape today.

The Rabbits

for Sue Buchanan

It's easier before the snow —
O the green fields of Eden, O —
They make their run, and down they go.

Once all the time was smooth and slow,
Plenty to eat, not much to know:
It's easier before the snow.

Later the games, the speed, the show,
The sense of life risked on a throw:
They make their run and down they go.

The mating of the buck and doe
All of that kind old so-and-so —
It's easier before the snow.

Some creatures just seed down and grow.
These creatures are all heel and toe —
They make their run and down they go.

Light breaks a little world in two:
The gasp, the sudden vertigo:
It's easier before the snow.
They make their run, and down they go.

One and One

for Peter Pierce

Having reached a flat point in the meandering story
that he was constructing — he called it a *bildungs-roman*
though he had no German and little other learning —

he met precisely the figure he needed: a divorcee,
a witty, worldly, somewhat disillusioned woman,
sexually awakened, frustrated now, slow-burning.

She had admitted at last that bad beginnings
come true: the princess is stripped and whipped and
                        treated just like a person,
until, equally improbably, she is rescued

by a man who never played a straight bat, made a good innings,
who has slaughtered henwives, dwarves, committed arson,
looks overall stupid though lucky, anything but shrewd.

They love one another at once: how could they not do so?
Enraptured, he tells his story and she tells hers, and neither
notices the sheer difference of modes.

He plans a honeymoon in Arabia, she a trousseau
of velvet and lace: they have no common weather.
He likes elegies. She likes Pindaric odes.

Whether they marry or not, my gentle reader,
is hardly the point: the question is, would you rather
love in mutual delusion, nursing your silly stories,
or live in clear wit, alone with your cat and the furies?

What Happened Next

for Sue

When the lucky third son succeeded in keeping his counsel,
killed the dragon, married the princess,
he was still the lucky third son.

Set in the throne-room, he hated the silk and tinsel,
the weight of heir-looms made him die by inches,
he thought all the lackeys were trying to have him on.

Lucky as ever, kingship allowed him to
see whom he liked: he appointed a Royal Cobbler,
a Royal Wheel-wright, a Royal Cabinet-maker —

to do him the justice no-one else will do,
he chose them himself, there was no committee nobbler —
and at last a Royal Poet, a sorry old wise-acre.

In a way, after that, his reign was happy enough:
he had hours and hours of course of Council meetings
to sit through each week, but one thing he was was patient:

he remembered his left and his right, he never talked tough,
he was never remiss in sending condolences, greetings,
and little cards of awe to the very ancient.

Sometimes, however, he forgot his origins,
thought himself really master of the court
and offered with a peasant son's largesse

over-sized slugs of whisky, martinis, pink gins
to his humble cronies, calling them *mate* and *sport*.
It made all sense of precedence a mess.

He didn't ever, have an idea in the head
so soon chopped off by his courtiers. Once he was dead
a new dragon flapped up to the castle, screaming to be fed.

Back to the cold transparent ham again

('Sonnet to Vauxhall')

Light years and half a world away
from Vauxhall Gardens, Hood's closure rings true:
    after the pyrotechnics, back
to cold comfort. But somewhere in lost time
    the patterned illuminations
hang in their perfect suspension, blue for
    memory, red for desire.

More colours: more colours shone in
those delicate globes of coruscation set
    against the dark to mimic
the wheeling unseen order of the stars,
    too bright, too evanescent for
mimesis, too clear to be forgotten.
    They had a God-be-with-you look.

Back to the cold transparent ham
again. Comedy is with us always,
    common-sense re-asserts itself:
they mount, they shine, evaporate, and fall.
    Mundanity, quotidian
ways of the world obtrude; but somewhere else
    the traceries of light burn on.

The Enchanted Present: a Ballade

Another time had other tales to tell,
another space had other figures for them:
should the sad sorcerers swim up to here from hell
I'm sure I'd have the spirit to abhor them,
if not the wit to scatter them and score them.
In other places, sorcerers abound
and people both placate them and deplore them.
Here only Susie makes my eyes grow round.

How the grim riders rake across the fell!
How princesses, with princes to adore them,
spring up enchanted from each broken spell!
Alas, sad shepherd, safely you ignore them,
who with your woolly ways would blind and bore them,
sitting bewildered on your little mound.
I understand, of course: I never saw them:
here only Susie makes my eyes grow round.

How dark and deep the secrets of a well,
how strange the fates of those who would explore them!
What loathly, crafty genii loci dwell
in mountain caves, and in the coombs before them!
Wonderful webs they wove before they tore them —
where every footpath led to hallowed ground,
how much our silly elders had to awe them!
Here only Susie makes my eyes grow round.

l' Envoi

Prince, we have dwarves and wizards as we draw them,
drawing from stories that can still astound;
but as for magic robes, I never wore them.
Here only Susie makes my eyes grow round.

Anyway

If it were true that all true loves were false,
what could I do but love you anyway?
I can imagine loving no-one else.

The rhythms, the seductions of a waltz
might have a whole soul's being in their sway
if it were true that all true loves were false,

but given all the dances and their pulse,
the social steps, the changes and the play,
I could imagine loving no-one else.

The music might be Bach, the last schmaltz,
tears for tomorrow, or for yesterday:
if it were true that all true loves were false

it wouldn't matter, matter in the least,
the bands might play whatever they might play.
I can imagine loving no-one else —

which seems as quaint, as old-fashioned as chintz.
In a fake world, might one unfalsely say
if it were true that all true loves are false
what could I do but love you anyway?

Thinking of Suicide

for Dinny O'Hearn

Sitting alone over late dinner with wine
he remembers, I threatened suicide once.
The thoughts run on: I did it just to bully,
neither was I believed — it was no dunce
yielding to that importunate way of mine.
Some doubt remains: in that long-buried rhapsody
which voices cried how high, how loud, O will he, will I,
was anything at all in jeopardy?
Lost in the past, it sinks to sullen shame; and yet
further thoughts follow: was it from this that he
turned brutally to the common-sense belief
that threats of suicide are always merely threat
— *unless you love me, you will be brought to grief,*
stricken for years by what you would not offer me —
and best ignored in a well-meaning way?
Another glass of wine. Older, he cannot say,
can only be grateful that no-one ever took
him for that sort of loved-one, lover. Look,
I'm not like that. Five minutes to the beach:
he thinks of walking down, his clothes in a small pile,
swimming a steady breaststroke under the half moon
until cold water puts him out of reach.
Only a passing thought: it makes him smile
as Handel strikes out on a glorious tune.
It's getting rather cold, it's rather late.
No-one is there to watch him as he licks his plate.

Insomnia

For Alan Davies

There are two kinds of sleeplessness. One is mean:
you lie there with your eyes shut, and things war
in endless repetition, racing, in dull white.
Or you might lie there, patient, wide-eyed in the dark,
thinking the same things over and over with a dull peace,
resigned to the resolution of day-break.

Grace save us from racing thoughts: they always break
down to one question: *what did she (or he, or it,*
                    even they) really mean?
Dialogues are remembered, dismembered piece by piece,
yielding nothing but the sense of a last sad war
where all you want is to wave a flag of white,
to have it stop, to be gone into simple dark.

Insomniacs, bless them, are never afraid of the dark:
bad nights are called 'white nights' for that dull white
which lurks behind their eye-lids, dingy, mean,
nothing at all like innocence, purity or peace,
signalling that all the nerves would like to break.
Something in the whole being is at war,

but whatever war it is, it's an undeclared war,
and whatever might ensue, it won't be peace
unless with the clarity of saintliness or heart-break,
whatever either or both of those words might mean,
someone or something from another and certain dark
is able somehow to offer a glimpse of unsullied white.

41

I lie at ease these nights in fields of white,
thinking of this and that, murmuring in the dark,
convalescent perhaps from a younger war:
I think of gain and loss, of how things grow and break:
I think of meanings, what my meanings mean,
and counting words can almost count myself at peace.

But who else asks no more than singular peace?
All the bright strainers yearning towards day-break
are coining messages, slogans against the dark
to break into the rainbow that they want from white.
Some will make love: they and others will make war:
generous, self-seeking, high-minded, vague, and mean.

There will be no golden mean, however things might break:
there is going to be more war, much of it in the dark:
there will also be unsullied white and drifts of peace.

Three Poems
For My Daughters

A Jig for Kate

My Kate she is a gormish girl —
which way will you turn lass:
with an Irish jig down the yellow brick road
to Melbourne town when the world was young
and the bay a forest of masts?
To a marvellous run on the Darling Downs,
cantering, cantering — easy now,
hold tight while it lasts
with a hop, a skip and a twirl
and let the ladies pass.
  The ladies in their satins and bows
  to the fiddle and concertina
  walked off the ships, and then God knows
  how they managed their proud demeanour.

My Kate she is a gormish girl —
which way will you turn lass:
with hardly a glance down a glassy road
as everything dwindles out of sound
and under the lenses swim
thingumajigs neither loving nor knowing,
growing, shrinking, changing skins,
neither unhappy nor dim
in their creaturely swirl
under a neutral glass?

The ladies in their masks and capes
walk out and in through sucking doors
between the amoebae and the apes,
gracefully, without applause.

My Kate she is a gormish girl —
what way will you turn lass:
with your feet so quick and your hands just so
and the sky and houses all around,
people near and far;
with a world still waiting to be made
and you so deft and sure and slow and
O! how the chances jar . . .
 With the ladies neat and the ladies loose,
 ladies dumb and ladies clever,
 ladies everything — Goodness knows
O! it's a way, it's a world
in which things pass, things pass
 this might go on forever.

Summer Days with Daughter

Was she made after all
to laugh and fall in water?
We played at catching ball —
"harder", she called back, "harder",

and so I'd throw it higher,
wider, slower, faster:
all this occasioned laughter,
astonishing quickness, skill.

On dry land who more loveable
than Rachel at eleven,
solicitous of her father?
I can't imagine, even.

Goose Girl

for Myfanwy

The princess is out at grass with geese,
ill-mannered hauteur keeps the throne.
No horse's head will speak its piece:
one is one, and all alone.
How should you win the world's regard?
Gentleness is its own reward.

In fairy-tales, all ends are true:
in common life there is no end —
only geese gobbling at the grass,
a girl who sees the traffic pass,
keeping an imagined friend,
speaking when she's spoken to.

The seasons change, the geese take flight,
winging in skeins across the sky
from here to there, wherever and why,
showing scarcely a trace of doubt.
They know the way they have to go.
I'm learning, and you might learn too.

Shadows of the night are falling —
what am I doing, calling my darling
a precious goose that's out at grass;
where has the princess flown, alas?
Somewhere beyond the world's regard:
gentleness is its own reward.

The Clerk's Petition

for Peter Steele, S.J.

When the world finally
disappears under
a flood of fouled paper,
let me not, lord,
be deemed to have done
much more than my share,
all too uncalled-for.

High Summer

a cry of absence, absence in the heart
                    — Ransom

In the blaze of noon, I am burnt;
pages flick over and over:
something is being learned.

Sometimes I crawl for cover.
More often, though, I head
for the great flux and hover

over the ambience we fled
lucky, unlucky aeons ago.
I might as well be dead —

but while the world is hot and safe and slow
living is easy. Just another dip.
Now where did all the others go?

They're always giving me the slip.
I shall be done to a turn
when we all meet on Charon's boat.

A Solicitors' World

for Linton Lethlean

A world of lunches, conferences behind
    locked doors, negotiations
balanced on wheedling, common-sense, sometimes
    something like threat, and running
on money, which after all it burns up
    faster than anything else,
when it turns its face to the light it blinks
    and hoots, owl-like, about Justice.

Who knows more about justice than this does?
    A thousand years have fed it
conundrums to codify, precedents
    for every human failing:
no wonder therefore, alas, that it should
    grunt, gurgle, and grind most things
down to a sorry slurry: from the law
    only lawyers do well. Well,

not quite: though broad enough a target for
    satire's blindest archer, this
also is a shield beneath which huddle
    misery's people, many
against all odds offered understanding,
    lenity, not always fleeced.
Not a world I wish to be embroiled in,
    yours is a world that yields men

I would sooner talk to than most.

49

Mr Todd

for the Connor coven

The foxes are taking over the suburbs —
in England, that is. Here they're too sly to be seen,
except perhaps in a certain way with adverbs,
a glimpse of reddish-brown through the common green.

Foxes take care of their own, which is what they're there for:
and a fox knows his own, by night even more than by day.
A fox has an awful lot to care for:
alone, he knows his bounds, and does not stray.

Will there be goose for Christmas? He will be there
counting his little ones, eight nine ten . . .
Not only foxes care, but foxes care
about their grounds, the fastness of their den.

Soldier's Heart*

for the chaps

Sometimes I'm short of puff,
sometimes I bark a bit;
not really very tough,
I'm more than half-way fit.

Some of it was exciting,
lots of mines and flares:
there was a bit of fighting —
since we're together now, who cares?

No more parades, thank God:
top brass and high noon are done.
With all you odds and sods
I'll just keep soldiering on.

* (Soldier's Heart . . . or Effort Syndrome,
is a term applied to a set of
symptoms . . . consisting of palpitation,
shortness of breath, speedy
exhaustion, depression and irritability.
The condition also occurs in civil
life, but received its name on
account of the frequency with which
it was noticed during the 1914–18
War. — Black's Medical Dictionary.)

Children's Games

for Peter Steele, SJ

Rich man, poor man, beggarman, thief,
king of the mountain, running the gauntlet,
oats and beans and barley grow, the farmer takes a wife.

Musical chair's, crack-the-whip, hopscotch, hunt-
                             the-thimble,
Postman's knock, three blind mice, handy-dandy, tipcat,
blindman's buff, odds and evens, Frau Rose, Jack be
                             nimble.

Ricketty Kate, mumblety-peg, prisoner's base, *my word*,
happy families, bounce the baby, Jack and Jill and
                             solo,
stumblers on the way to meet the lord.

Swan Song

for Alan Davies

Ugly and maladroit, I hardly noticed when
shy as a father, you,
seeing the goose in the gosling,
first offered me your wing.

Still, it was nice to follow
the crazy paths you made
through the ubiquitous duckweed
on which I fed.

Trade winds blew off course.
A young Cob yearns to find
A Pen that he can live with.
I almost lost my mind.

Study of the Anatidae
suggests that swanning on,
stylish once in most resorts,
is now a dying game.

Sheer elegance and little brains:
we've had enough of these.
Good luck to you as the world turns over:
May all your swans prove geese.

Ecce Homo

I.M. David Fitts, 1946–1980

Not everything is well:
broken on the wheel
you too abruptly fell.

After the long-weekend
in which I harrowed Hell,
I was up and about.

Grand Illusion

for Peter Porter

Beguiled by patter, card-tricks,
passes with silver rings, silk scarves,

we sit through thunder and incense
to boggle at large illusions:

aha, aha, how the audience
gasps as a pachydern goes

abruptly from plain sight;
and oho how the lovers of cats

sigh as a tiger burns up in a hoop,
the pride of lions flickers and goes out;

and when at last the gold-spangled girl
is slowly cut into halves,

hurrah, hurrah cry the little children,
so singular themselves.

Aha indeed, and oho and hurrah:
for when the brilliant lights go down

and all the little lights say *Exit*,
everything's as it was, or ought to be:

the great cats skulk in their cages,
the elephant is tethered in the lane.

But where is the lady I came in with,
she whom I shall never see again?